ARE YOU A BULLYRAG?

Naughty Or Nice

KATHELINE TATE

AuthorHouse™
1663 Liberty Drive
Bloomington, IN 47403
www.authorhouse.com
Phone: 1 (833) 262-8899

Because of the dynamic nature of the Internet, any web addresses or links contained in this book may have changed since publication and may no longer be valid. The views expressed in this work are solely those of the author and do not necessarily reflect the views of the publisher, and the publisher hereby disclaims any responsibility for them.

Any people depicted in stock imagery provided by Getty Images are models, and such images are being used for illustrative purposes only.
Certain stock imagery © Getty Images.

Scripture quotations marked KJV are from the Holy Bible, King James Version (Authorized Version). First published in 1611. Quoted from the KJV Classic Reference Bible, Copyright © 1983 by The Zondervan Corporation.

This book is printed on acid-free paper.

ISBN: 978-1-7283-4379-2 (sc)
ISBN: 978-1-7283-4378-5 (e)

Library of Congress Control Number: 2020901208

Print information available on the last page.

Published by AuthorHouse 08/15/2020

authorHOUSE

PREFACE

Have you ever felt afraid, lonely or rejected?

Do you ever feel that you lose control when someone teases you?

Do you feel as though you are a target of being mistreated by others?

Do you feel powerless and want to control or dominate others?

If you answered yes to any one of these questions, then this book is definitely one that you should read because it will help you feel better about yourself and help you find your special place in the world.

I wrote this book because as retired educator over the years I have witnessed many incidents of students and others who have felt rejected, humiliated and insecure because people have treated them in an unkind manner.

Sometimes, a sneer, a look or unkind word can cause someone to feel rejected.

Bullying is an age - old problem and a menace to other people. People who bully others are often afraid of something, feel lonely and rejected. It is possible that they might have other negative behavior problems that cause them to bully others.

Sometimes, bullies are insecure about themselves, have a low self-ego and fight these insecurities by causing others to feel insecure of fearful. Bullyrags tend to try to control or dominate others by teasing or bullying another person. They are looking for a way to feel powerful and controlling of others.

If you are a target of a bullyrag, do not blame yourself. You are a unique person with a special physical appearance, disability, interests, race or sexuality. Learn to accept your unique characteristic and never yield to a bullyrag. Remember that you are the powerful one and the bullyrag is powerless and weak.

There are many more similarities than differences in people. You can find them and learn to accept others as God made them.

INTRODUCTION

Genesis 1: 1-2

"In the beginning, God created the heaven and the earth. And the earth was without form and void, and darkness was upon the face of the deep. And the spirit of God moved upon the face of the waters. "And God said, "Let there be light and there was light.

And God saw that the light, that it was good and God divided the light from darkness. And God called the light Day and the darkness He called night, and the evening and the morning were the first day." And God continued to create animals in the sea, fowl in the air and more animals and plants on the earth.

Genesis 1:26

"And God said, "Let's make man in our own image, after our likeness and let them have dominion over the fish of the sea and over the fowl of the air and over the cattle and over all the earth and over every creeping thing that creeps upon the earth.

Genesis 1:27-28

So, God created man in His own image, in the image of God, created He him; male and female created He them.

DEDICATION

Dedicated to my wonderful parents and grandparents who taught me to be kind and loving to others and to respect and obey the Golden Rule, "Do unto others as you would have them do unto you."

To all of the wonderful teachers at Charles M. Hall School in Alcoa, Tennessee, who stressed the importance of being kind and loving to others.

To all of the Pastors, youth leaders and people in my community who taught me and others to practice the teaching of love and respect that God has for all people. People in my community interacted with the children and parents to help teach them the importance and value of respecting and showing love to others.

This concept follows a famous African proverb from the Nigerian Igbo Culture, Oran a azu nwa' which means, "It takes a village or community to raise a child.

And

To anyone who has been made to feel lonely, sad, unappreciated, ridiculed and inferior because of a Bullyrag.

I am wonderfully made.

Made in the image of God.

God loves me, even with my big nose and big ears.

My big nose is better for smelling Grandma's chocolate cookies, the aroma of her rolls, corn bread and pound cake.

My big ears are better for hearing my favorite music, like classical, jazz, gospel, and even country music.

And for listening to the Pastor's sermon on Sunday morning.

Big ears are good for hearing my Mother say, "Close the refrigerator door" or stop running in the house and I love you".

Big and little ears are great for listening to Mother read aloud stories.

My big ears can hear the birds singing, the crickets chirping and if I am very still, I can hear a word from God.

I wear glasses and I sometimes I am called, four eyes. I can see how to read much better and I like looking at the colors of a rainbow. Four eyes are better for me to see you when you smile.

My glasses help me see the smallest ant on a leaf in my Mother's garden.

And………. the butterflies colors are brighter, too.

When I open these big eyes, I see all the beauty around me, beautiful flowers, a beautiful sunrise and the great big sun that is warming the earth.

In the evening, I can see a beautiful sunset, later at night, I can see the beautiful moon and stars in the sky. I can even see the Big and Little Dipper on a clear night.

God still loves me and I love you, too.

I love you even when you tease me about my size 13 shoe,

But............... Let me tell you, my big feet can help me jump really high,

I can hike eight miles on the trail in the Great Smoky Mountains in Tennessee and on the Appalachian Trail.

My big foot can kick a football almost to the goal post.

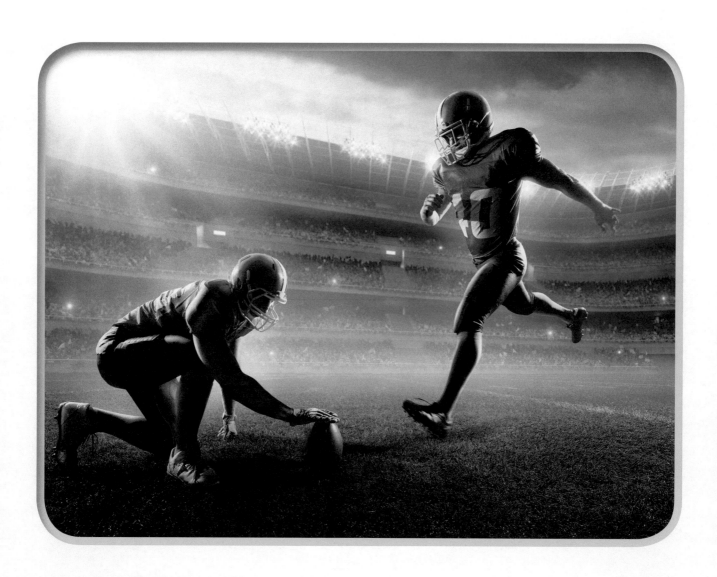

My extra-large hands can reach across all of the keys on my piano.

And my tiny fingers can push the buttons on the keyboard of my computer, play a clarinet and the trumpet.

My dark skin is smooth, beautiful and shiny, like a sparkling diamond.

God still loves me and I love you because I am made in the image of God.

You can write your own thoughts on this page.

My curly, thick, braided hair, is so beautiful and I can style it in so many ways.

And some will ask, "How do you do it?"

I never tell because it is my secret and that is the truth.

You and I look amazingly beautiful.

My fair skin and straight blonde hair are beautiful, too.

I guess it is just in my genes, some say I look exactly like my Mother's Aunt, who lives in Switzerland.

I think I was just made in the image of God,

He loves me and I love you, too.

My brother has red hair, full of thick curls.
Looks like a carrot in a vegetable garden.
He is often teased and called Carrot Top Boy,
But God loves him and he loves you, too.

You can write your own thoughts on this page.

Gee, I almost forgot about my big forehead,

With the red pimples on it.

A hat fits this big forehead just right,

And with this hat on my big head,

the pimples will be out of sight.

Don't bully me! Look at yourself in the mirror.

Do you like what you see?

I am what I am and who I am,

God still loves me just as I am.

You can write your own thoughts on this page.

Freckles, Freckles, Freckles

Heckles, Heckles, Heckles.

For every freckle, there is a kind thought in my head, a soft spot in my heart and a kind word for you, too.

Yes, I am very tall, 7 feet, 4 inches tall, Tall enough to easily dunk a basketball.

My little sister is very short, but she can easily hide under the bed and no one can find her.

Now as for lips, some can be big, some small, but each kind whether big or small can sip a drink from a straw,

Whistle a tune, blow a bubble,
Kiss Mom and Dad goodnight.

Once someone said, "You are too skinny,"

I gained a few pounds

and someone else said, "You are too fat."

I wish they would make up their minds.

It really doesn't matter because I am who I am.

It takes all kind of people to make a world, big and little, fat and skinny, tall and short, all made by God.

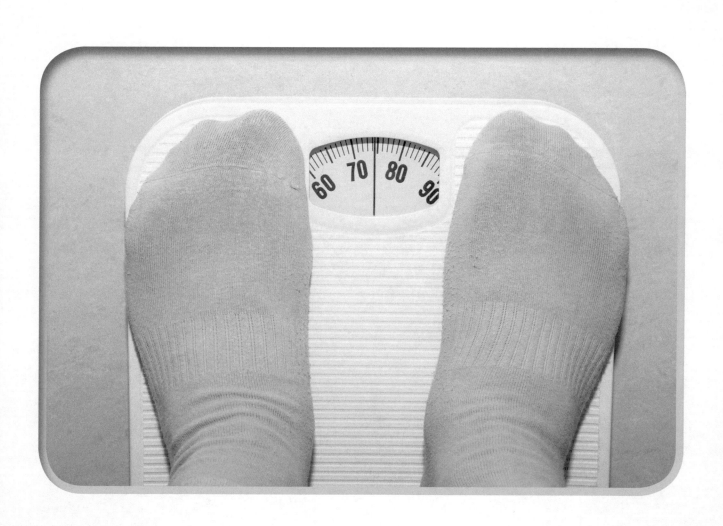

And I am in this world, too. Thinking and learning in a different way.

For you see, I am Autistic, but I am still made by God.

God loves me and I love you too.

I go to a special school and sometimes speak slowly,

and sound funny, too.

I am what you and some people call, "Mentally Challenged"

Or Autistic or I might have a learning disability.

Or I could have Tourette's or Down Syndrome
Or I am bald because I had cancer,
Yet, these things do not define me.

I am what I am because God made me.

I can do many things in a special class or a special school.

I like helping my Mom, so I wash the dishes and clean my room.

I help build cars at a car factory in my home town.

The boss says I do a good job and I get paid, too.

God still loves me and I love you, too.

When I was born, I looked like a boy so I was given a boy's name.

I had curly hair, my feet and hands are small and very dainty like a girl.

I never felt quite like a boy.

I liked to so do what some people said were "girl things" like playing with dolls, and wearing makeup.

I liked to sneak in my sister's room to put on different shades of eyeshadow but most of all I liked putting mascara on my long, beautiful eyelashes.

Often when no one was around, I liked to dance in my sister's high heeled shoes. Often, I felt out of place and wanted to be a real girl.

I was called names but I did not care. I knew that God still loved me because He made me, too.

You can write your own thoughts on this page.

There are many colors in the rainbow,

All made by God.

Before the great flood and even after the great flood,

God made a rainbow of people in His image.

Everyone was made by God, even You,

You can find something good in everyone,

So, Make the Pledge! No More Bullying! Don't Be A Bullyrag!

Printed in the United States
By Bookmasters